D0851104

Multiverses

poems by

Celia Lisset Alvarez

Finishing Line Press
Georgetown, Kentucky

Multiverses

ACKNOWLEDGMENTS

Version 0.0 appeared as "My Father Leaves Cuba" in *Iodine Poetry Journal*
Spring/Summer 2009.

Publisher: Leah Huete de Maines
Editor: Christen Kincaid
Cover Art: Baptism by Jonathan K. Rice
Author Photo: Celia Lisset Alvarez
Cover Design: Elizabeth Maines McCleavy

Order online: www.finishinglinepress.com
also available on amazon.com

Author inquiries and mail orders:
Finishing Line Press
P. O. Box 1626
Georgetown, Kentucky 40324
U. S. A.

Table of Contents

For Arturito,
all of them.

"This is the best of all possible worlds."

—Gottfried Leibniz, *Théodicée,* 1710

"You can't keep jumping from reality to reality in hopes of finding one that you can fix. Or one that is perfect for you. No reality is perfect. You're exactly where you're meant to be. You have to stand and face reality."

—M.K. Williams, *The Infinite-Infinite,* 2019

Version 1.00

In the NICU,
they try to reassure me
with stories of babies
born at 23 weeks
who have survived
just like you and I,
no mark of this struggle
of wires and buttons,
dials and digital heartbeats.

Born at 27 weeks, Arturo
is more fetus than baby.
I gasp the first time I see them,
my twins, Arturo and Sara.
In the violet light of the incubator,
I struggle to make out the color
of their hair or their eyes.
The only way I can tell them apart
is that Sara's hat has a jaunty bow.
Try to remain positive, they say.

They let me change their diapers.
Arturo's eyes slit slightly open,
flash of black, amphibious.
I give him the tip of my finger
and his hand curls around it,
like a kitten's paw. He is intubated,
the tape covering his lower face
like a mask. His chest is covered
by sensors. Even the preemie diaper
reaches to his armpits.

All that I can see,
because they cannot cover it
in order to have a place from which
to draw blood, is his left foot,
a bulbous big toe standing straight

up in the air, just like mine.
Just like mine. This is my son.

Even when the crash cart comes in,
even when I can no longer tell
which doctor can save him,
I believe that things will turn around.
When the beep of his heartbeat
goes silent, I clutch my husband and
watch my son turn purple, beginning
with his toe. This is my son,

I say to myself, when I
can finally hold him, free
from tubes and tape. I think
of the multiverse theory,
wondering what version of me
can hold him alive and breathing,
what version of me
can take him home,
can watch him grow.

Sara's hair is golden,
her eyes a streaming blue river.
She squeals with laughter
as my mother makes her
airplane sounds with her spoon.

I think of that version of me
where there are two toddlers,
skin so white you can see
their map of veins. I trace
Sara's blue highways to her
big toe, bulbous, alert, ready
to spring into action.

Version 2.00

The nurses clap and cheer
as I exit the NICU,
a baby in each arm
and one behind, now
"big" sister Lucy, still
just one.

We've gone into debt
to buy a Honda Odyssey,
the only minivan to fit
comfortably three carseats.

I wait by the curb on the street,
pink and blue balloons bouncing
from my wheelchair, and Rafael
pulls up, the proud papa, takes
a picture of us before we struggle
to get each baby in a carseat.

The Montes-Mobile,
we will call it, as well as the
three-seat stroller
I spent months researching,
finally settling on a train,
figuring that a side-by-side
would not maneuver well
down the aisles at Publix,
where little hands would
reach to grab a bright box
of cereal.

As we exit the hospital,
I look in the rear view mirror,
see the lunch lady that was
so nice, and I turn towards
the road home, only green
lights ahead, and behind me,

a cacophony of cries
I will have to find a way to soothe.

Anxious and weak,
I breathe in the whispering air
of the new van, and wonder
what version of me will be capable
of such work. How we will

eat, how we will sleep, how
we will bathe, how will I
coordinate such need—too many
questions. I settle

into the bucket seat of the van,
try to stockpile the comfort
I know I will lack
in the coming years. A mixture

of fear and joy propels us
into our cramped home,
where every corner
will soon be covered
with toys, diaper boxes,
teething rings, and pacifiers.

Version 1.05

I hold my purple baby in my arms
for a long time. An Episcopalian preacher
attempts to comfort me. *It's okay
to be angry,* he says, tears covering
his face. I feel the need to say
something.

The Catholic priest is long in coming.
My baby is cold and hard when he performs
whatever he performs. He leaves quickly.
Everyone hugs me.
They leave one by one.
I can hear them outside the room,
the only room my son ever saw.
I hear my mother's voice thanking
someone: *the coffee is good.*

It is only my husband and I,
and our dead purple baby. Our second
Arturo, the first a near-second trimester
miscarriage that we had already named
after my favorite uncle. We are told
we can stay as long as we want.
It is up to me to decide
when I've had enough
when I'm ready to put my baby
in the acrylic crib by the door, and
leave him there for other hands
to wheel him to the morgue.
I do not remember Sara is in the room.

In some days' time there will be a mass
and the gospel will read, *For God
so greatly loved and dearly prized the world
that He gave up His only begotten Son, so that
whoever believes in Him shall not perish
but have eternal life.*

I have given up my son Arturo to these rituals.
Now there are two graves marked Arturo Montes.
Somewhere in Avoca, New Jersey, the original
Arturo's ashes sit in his wife's family mausoleum.
There are no Arturos left.

I will not visit this new grave for a long time.
After 66 days, Sara will go home
with severe reflux, and there will be nights
when I will hold her very still, hoping
the formula I have painstakingly given
her four-pound body will stay inside her.
There is no sound when it
shoots out of her mouth across the room,
there is no sound
to my desperation
to the creeping suspicion
that perhaps I will have to give her up too.

I think about eternal life.
What version of my son will I encounter there?
Will he be forever a mess of tubes and tapes,
or perhaps, the purple fading into pink,
he will grow into a real baby. And what if

I live another 50 years? Will I find
a grown stranger in heaven
who will embrace me and call me mother?
None of these possibilities seem right.

I pray for Sara anyway.

Version 2.10

My father holds his grandson
for the first time.
Afraid of hospitals,
he did not witness
the terror of the machines
that one must watch,
constantly,
as if the watching
could somehow control
the readings.

No, he wasn't there
when the tube went down his
grandson's throat, when I
was taught to feed him
through his nose with a syringe.

The boy that he holds now is
small, but perfect, and though
his eyes are blue my brown-eyed father
sees himself in those clear eyes,
sees himself live on now
into a fuzzy future
where flying cars and computers
whizz his grandson to his job
as a lawyer or a doctor
quite frankly anything other
than what his only child became,
a poet he could not understand.

In his arms he finds release.
Now living or dying is the same.
Should he live, he'll live to see the day
Arturito—as he will of course be called,
the Spanish diminutive that plagued
my 97-year-old uncle to his grave—
he'll live to see the day Arturito

throws his first baseball. Or,
should he die, there will be baseball
anyway. Perhaps tennis.
He is free to do as he pleases.

They look into each other's eyes. There
is an instant bond that leaps far
over my head into the world they
happily belong to, the inaccessible
world of men another version of me
was perhaps able to puncture, my father
and I jumping to the beat of the dog races,
the clack of dominoes on the table,
the shots of the jai alai ball on the wall.

Version 3.00

The jelly is warm on my skin
as the tech moves the handle
of the ultrasound machine from
side to side. *It's a girl!* she says
with great enthusiasm. I see

a brief wave of disappointment
appear and then get hidden quickly
behind my husband's smile.
We already have a girl, and
I am old.
This is our last baby, and
there will be no son
to carry on his name,
to toss a football with,
to share a beer.
We think this is disappointment.

Another version of me
wonders what the point is
of coming into this world
only to be throttled by tubes
and pinched by needles
for 26 days, only to die
gasping for air.

But this other version
quickly adjusts. We toss
girl names at each other
on the way home. Lucy
is so small we still
have leftover names—
will it be Laura? Sara?

It is a seamless pregnancy.
There are no twins struggling for room
in my cramped uterus. Sara

does not kick her way out
of her amniotic sac 13 weeks
ahead of time.

We take good care of Lucy's clothes,
paint the new nursery's walls pink.

Version 1.10

The day of my son's burial
is bright and hot. Karina
takes Lucy in her arms.
Eddy has taken the day off
to be with us.

The minute it's over
I drive from the cemetery
straight back to the NICU.
They have moved Sara
to a different room
in a less critical
part of the hospital.

Nurses hug me and cry.
They make promises
about Sara. All I want

is to be left alone with her.
to be able to hold her
in my arms now that
it is possible, and sing
to her. I sing softly

the songs I know—
Mötley Crüe's "Home
Sweet Home." I hum

"Boadicea" by Enya and
think of the ancient British
queen, wishing her strength
upon Sara.

They call it kangaroo time—
whenever you carry your baby,
the mess of tubes dangling
from her arms, chest, legs,

spread out like a frog skin to skin.
The supposition is that my
body's warmth has some
magical properties that will
strengthen Sara. I rock and
rock her on the bulky armchair,
my shirt unbuttoned, my bra
no doubt rough against her skin.

The day Arturo died the incubator
was open when I came in
and he laid splayed out on the bed
like a starfish.
Some kind of infection was
ravaging his body.
His belly was as big as a baseball.

The last time I had kangarooed
him I had been uncomfortable
and wanted to put him back
in the incubator after just half
an hour. We took the only picture
we'd ever take together that day.
I worried about the two inches
of roots that showed at the part
in my hair. I did not sing to him.

After Boadicea lost the lands
she had regained from the Romans,
she died, likely poisoning herself.

At night when I go home
I start sleeping with my
earbuds on. The same songs
over and over and over.
I'm on my way, just set me free,
home sweet home.

Version 1.15

The night Arturo dies
my father is sleeping
when we get home.

In the morning before
the funeral, I expect
to see him drenched

in tears, ready to bemoan
the fact that he never
got to see his grandson,

how his own cowardice
kept him from the one
opportunity he would

ever have. Instead he
is silent as I pass behind
him, seated at the

breakfast table as if
this were any morning.
Though he attends

the mass, the funeral,
and the burial, he says
not one word to me

for thirty days. Coming
home one night from
the NICU where Sara

somehow still survives,
he surprises me by the
door, hugs me awkwardly,

his voice cracking as he

says *you know I'm no good*
at this sort of thing and

the fact that it was the boy—
he trails off into a little moan
and shuffles back into his

room. I stand there wondering
if my mother has prodded him
into saying something. I

imagine another version
of the scene, one in which
we hug one another fiercely.

so fiercely, and I say
Papi, Papi, my little boy
turned purple and died.

In another version, I push
him away violently, so very
violently, and I scream

You're too late! Too late.
Too late. You missed your
one shot. And now you

must forever live with that.
But in this version, in this
version I turn off the living

room light, microwave
something to eat,
and go to sleep.

Version 2.30

My father becomes
a wonderful babysitter
he deftly maneuvers
the Montes-Mobile
(the stroller, not the minivan)
down the street,
greeting the neighbors
he never got to know
before he retired.

They ask about Lucy
and the twins and my father
dabs his forehead with his
handkerchief, complaining
about his lack of stamina
to keep up with them
at such an advanced age.

The neighbors encourage him.
Pancho, they say, you should
realize how lucky you are
to be able to wheel such a heavy load
all the way down the road.

Version 2.20

I wake up at 5 am.
I change Arturito's diaper first,
the way Nurse Bianca taught me—
unfasten the diaper and quickly
open and close it, because the
feel of the air is what makes them
pee. Then Sara.

I've bought a special recliner
and a special twin pillow.
I hold each baby under an arm
like a football, and they
breastfeed at the same time.
I keep a bottle of water
by my side to avoid dehydration.

After I lull them back to sleep
I wake Lucy for potty time. It's
early to start training her at
eighteen months, but I've googled strategies
that work. I need her to be able to do this
so I can concentrate on the twins.
After potty time I give her breakfast,
and she can already feed herself.
After that I will put her back in her crib
and let her watch cartoons—bad parenting,
I know, but it's time for the twins' next feeding.

All day long my every minute is
calculated. There must be as few
changes as possible—one trip
to the doctor and I'm thrown off.

You're handling it so well,
my friends say on the phone,
and though I complain, I am
secretly pleased. I have prepared

myself well—months of research:
I know to pump after every feeding
so I can sleep at night
while Rafael takes over.
I know just what to eat and
how much water to drink
for maximum milk production.
I have an entire notebook
with bullet points, tips, and schedules.

An entire notebook. Months of work
preparing for this moment, making every
effort to be prepared
for any contingency.

Version 3.1

We are in the elevator at Whole Foods
when the nice American lady asks
the inevitable question:
Are these the only children you have?

People always assume there's one
off at college somewhere, and the girls
are some last-minute IVF attempts
to save our pointless marriage.

Another popular scenario is when
strangers compliment Rafael, whose
beard has gone white,
for his beautiful granddaughters.
These spur him to dye his beard—
a tragic event where his skin becomes
brown and the hair remains white.
He shaves off the white parts,
attempting to sport a very hipster goatee,
but the dyed skin beneath
makes him look like Fred Flintstone.

At night I stare at myself in the
bathroom mirror, scrutinizing my face
for signs of age. I have not gotten
the grandmother compliment—not yet.
I research soaps and toners, serums
and oils, eye creams and moisturizers.
My bedtime routine takes so long
Rafael comes to call it my *Cirque du Face.*
Every night as I exfoliate and moisturize
I chide myself for our long wait.
When we finish our PhDs.
When we get good steady jobs.
When we get a house of our own.
One morning I was suddenly thirty-six.
The next I was forty.

I can't help but think something
is missing, some bungle in our past
that would have turned out differently
with the flap of a butterfly's wings.
Some version of our family in
some alternate universe
where I am a young mother
surrounded by three smiling children.

Version 1.20

My father wants to be
with the girls all the time,
even though Lucy can't
be contained in her walker
anymore and he's too afraid
to pick up Sara.

Lucy climbs on the back
of the sofa and my mother screams.
There is a lot of screaming.

Soon after we find out my dad
has Alzheimer's. Not even mild,
but sort of mid-range. The
neurologist insists we shouldn't worry—
at his age something else will take him
before it gets bad.

I wonder what that could mean
and soon I get an answer.
He becomes paranoid. We are
conspiring against him to keep
the girls away (which is true,
since he takes to not bathing
or changing his diaper, the result
of years of incontinence). He believes
we are taking his money and threatens
to cash in his life insurance
and get us all. I start to talk about
lawyers and legal forms to render
my own father incompetent.

Nevertheless Lucy loves him,
her Pop-Pop who watches
cartoons in Spanish with her
and attempts to read her books.
I notice he has trouble remembering

words. Plane, he says, pointing
at a picture of a bird.

He almost faints during Sara's
first birthday party. I blame the
beer and margaritas he's been
chugging—he thinks—behind
my back. There is a picture of
all of us with him seated, his head
leaning against my arm. My lips
are pursed, furious. He is ruining
the Cinco-de-Mayo themed party
I've been planning for months,
with a memorial mass for Arturito
in the morning hardly anyone attends.

How come we can never take
one of those family portraits
where everyone's eyes are open,
and no one is forcing a smile?
Is there no fixing us?

I wonder how far back we'd have to go
to reach the point where everything
went wrong, where we deviated to this place
where I sit crying in the bedroom alone,
eating a stale piece of cake.

Version 1.30

The visit to Arturo's grave
the next day is anticlimactic.
His sister sits on the grass
and I wonder if there is such a thing
as prenatal memory. In the hospital,

during the three weeks I spent
on bedrest trying not to give birth,
the monitors would show their heartbeats
in perfect synchronicity. Though they each
had their own amniotic sac, they lay
like kidneys, head-to-head, Sara
upside-down, double dreaming.

Lucy runs downhill too far away
from us. My mother waits in the car,
the hill too steep for her to climb.

It should be peaceful here,
the nuns buried at the bottom of the hill,
the babies at the top, a marble Pietà
somewhat of a distraction from the construction
of a new plot getting dug in the back.
But it's not. It's hot and buggy and—
I want to go.

We lay flowers and say prayers to both
Arturos. No visiting my grandmother
today—too hot to walk to the mausoleum.
My uncle Manolo is too far away, in a plot
close to where we'll be, Rafael and I
and my parents, the four of us side by side
and on top of each other
as we were in life.

I feel nothing here.
Instead, I see Arturito

running down the slope of the hill
behind Lucy, a mess of blond curls
glimmering in the sun. I see him
seated next to Sara, the two of them
babbling in a language only they
can understand.

But underground, all decomposed?
a tethered soul clinging to this mother
who never sang him to sleep or fed
him from her breasts? Oh, this is
not the place, not the place.
Nowhere is. No amount of beautiful
flowers can mask the odor of death
that lingers in the air like a hot mist,
strangling every breath. *Let's go,*

I say, back to a version of ourselves
that we've constructed, stoic and solid
as stones. We have survived this.

So why must I sleep with my earbuds on,
wake up every morning to the maw
of the double doors of the NICU opening
and the room I never left?

Version 1.21

I catch my father giving Lucy
a bite of his ham sandwich.

Papi! I scream, *how many times
must I tell you we are vegan
and plan to raise the girls to be as well?*

It's just a little piece, he says,
and I go on a rant: *it's a matter of respect,
you don't respect our choices
just like you don't respect our privacy.*
(He's been peeking through the curtain
on the French door that separates
our side of the house from theirs,
trying to get a glimpse of the girls
when they are with us.)

Meanwhile Lucy chews and smiles
at her Pop-Pop as I whisk her away,
furious, too furious really, this one
piece of ham carrying the weight
of my whole upbringing, of an
entire lifetime of peeking through
my curtains and questioning my choices.

Just before I get to the door,
I put Lucy down and easily rip
off the curtain, a flimsy, dirty thing
I had once helped my mom put up
myself with two simple rods
and four small screws.

There, I think,
*now there'll be no more peeking,
no more pretending that there's
some kind of boundary to our
daily lives.*

I put Lucy in the crib next to Sara
and cry miserably on the bed
just like I did that night when I
was fifteen and they wouldn't
let me go out with Jorge Guerrero.

I marvel at the time tunnel I've
created, the Charybdis that has
swallowed me, the open maw
of the NICU doors.

You try to swim against the current,
exhaust yourself, and die.
Lucy's large enough to scramble
out of the crib. I find her face and hands
pressed against the door, my father
on the other side, blowing kisses
at each other while Lucy cries,
Pop-Pop. Pop-Pop. Pop-Pop.

Version 2.40

The first time we take the twins to the beach
it takes us half an hour to unpack the van:

the large comforter on which we will sit.
the two umbrellas to make enough shade,

Lucy's sand toys, creams and water bottles
for all of us, my mother's folding chair.

Lucy takes to the water right away, like she does
all things, going in headfirst and coming out

the other side laughing. Sara sits by the shore,
playing with pebbles. Arturito is more intrepid—

he's taking his first steps, legs splayed open
like a cowboy. He brings me a pink whelk shell

and I say *gimme a kiss*, which he does unabashedly,
pursing his lips and extending his neck. Rafael

swings Lucy high above his head and she splashes
down, down, and for a millisecond my heart stops,

but up she comes, blowing bubbles and laughing.
Again, again, she begs. My mother sits next to Sara

in her straw hat, and together they draw lines in the sand
that fill with clear water when the waves come in.

I am sure every person on the beach stops by
to congratulate us on our beautiful family,

offer us advice about the twins' delicate skin.
But I've got them covered from the tips of their heads

down to their bulbous toes in broad-spectrum,
waterproof, sweatproof, lifeproof SPF 50.

Version 0.50

But Arturito, I argue, *it's really*
no big deal. Lucy is two months
old and more than ready for
her first plane ride—

No, no, he argues, *you can't put a baby*
on a plane at that age, with
all those germs in the recirculating
air. I will see you in March

when you come visit me in
Sarasota. Besides, do you know
how much the plane ride is
from Miami to Raleigh? No, no.

Absolutely not. Which is when
perhaps I should have stopped
arguing, because I know that
when he gets to *absolutely*

there is no moving him. *I could drive*
to Orlando where we can stop for a breath.

An interstate drive with a baby?
he asks. *That's not safe.*

I'm beginning to think you don't
want to see me.

No, no, Lisset—a name only family
calls me—*how could you think such a thing?*

Don't you want to meet Lucy?

Oh, for heaven's sake, I can hear
his wife Lois say, *babies aren't*
even that interesting at that age.

She's being crazy.

You're being crazy, Arturito says, and I know
the battle is lost. School starts in August,
and Lucy'll go to daycare while I
go back to work. I will have to wait
until spring break to see him.

Version 0.43

I get the call to tell me I'm pregnant
at work, and Maria, my boss, becomes

the first to know. After near ten years
of trying, I feel nothing but relief.

My husband is more cautious. *Let's
not tell anyone just yet, let's enjoy*

the secret. I agree. But after the next
ultrasound, I hand my mother a glass

of whiskey, and say, *You're going to
need this.* She tells my dad and through

the door I hear him ask, *how old
is Lisset?* But I was prepared for that.

I revel in the things I allow myself to eat—
apple pie from Burger King (which is

accidentally vegan) and ice cream,
hot dogs and garlic fries dripping with grease.

One day I feast on falafel and fries,
followed by a nap. I wake up to pee

and there, on my panties, is bright red
blood. I start to scream—*call Whitley*

(our nurse), Rafael thinks 911. We
wind up in the car, and in the ER

an ultrasound reveals a chorionic
hematoma, a common cause of

first trimester bleeding. *You're*

still a mother, the tech whispers, while I

hear Arturito's heart beating like a train.
They put me on bedrest, which is fine,

because it's summer. I binge-watch
Flip or Flop and munch on carrots

and hummus, terrified of any meal
over 500 calories. Every time I need

to go to the bathroom I have to psych
myself. *You're still a mother,* I whisper

over and over. Within two weeks
the cramps begin. I find myself

calmly telling Rafael it's time
to go back to the ER. In the car

the cramps get so strong I scream.
This time the tech can find no heartbeat.

For two weeks I wait to see if somehow
she was wrong, until finally the doctor

convinces me it's over. A missed abortion.
Sometime before classes ended, I had gone

to check my hCG levels, and after that I'd bought
a pair of brown flats. *Arturito made me do it,*

I'd said to Rafael when I got home. *How do you know
it's a boy?* he'd asked, to which I had

responded, *I just do.* And he was,
he was, and my uncle Arturito never knew.

Version 0.44

According to the doctor, you were nothing but
a chemical mass of cells. Not even really
an embryo. Failure. Rejection. Did you have a soul?

Was that soul inside me the night
we went looking at the graffiti murals in Midtown?
Were there two of us walking in the dark,
gazing up at the dazzling walls, marveling
at the depth and breadth and height
monstrous men and women,
geometric figures, homages to Wilma Flintstone,
LeBron James, and Bob Marley?

A cement-block geography of pop, Miami's pink guts
rendered in swathes of primary colors and tagged
indecipherably by artists smart enough
to know that what matters is the art.

What part of you is visible in the picture
we took in front of the 10-foot insect woman,
tendrils of her hair glistening in silver spray paint
under the streetlights. I search my face,
my picture-smile, always so contrived.
Is there some trace on my lips of you,
a seed already curling into a tadpole?

The baby website says you had a dividing
heart, chambers getting ready to beat and pump blood.
I had signed up for the November birth club,
and they still send me their hapless bulletins,
trying to tell me what's going on in my uterus this week.

How much of you is left in me now
that I've bled out your nonlife, nonsoul, chemical self?

When I go back to Midtown the insect woman mural
is gone, some robot-future in blacks and reds

in her place, some dystopian vision.

They do that sometimes, paint over the murals.
No trace left of the art underneath, that other painter
who spent God knows how very long dreaming, planning,
measuring, coloring the vast canvas of the city
and then standing back—maybe only for
a moment—in that mute blush of satisfaction
invisible in the deep, black, empty night.

Version 0.45

Don't write about the moon,
no one wants to hear such triteness
how these images the doctor hands
me of my uterus, these mauve circles
on a black background
could be night scenes,
blood moons, romantic or gothic.

Now everything inside me is clean,
sterile. I am a perfect before and after.
A pink wash
trickles down my legs in the shower.
I am ready to be new
after the bleeding.

Don't write about the moon,
no matter how tempting the similarities,
the waxing and the waning,
the constant pulling out into space.
No one wants to hear about how I feel
tethered to something far away and cold,
airless, how it calls me. This is why
wolves howl, why it bothers us even
when we know
that we are safe,
that no one's coming for Red Riding Hood
or the Three Little Pigs.
No one wants to hear these Henny Penny complaints
about how the moon might come crashing down
someday, a fiery ball in the sky
no one will anticipate.

Version 0.46

*Los ojos de los axolotl me decían de la presencia de
una vida diferente, de otra manera de mirar.*
        –Julio Cortázar

This grief has separated us.
I have mutated like a fish,
grown gills to breathe this toxic air.
How ghastly.

You cannot understand
why I will not cover them,
why, in fact, I stretch my neck
like a balloon, miles above you.

I say *the air is thin here, full
of moisture.* I see you mouthing
a reply, down there, flailing
your arms. Unrecognizably small.

For my birthday
you have bought me a bright blue scarf.
It is the gift of a child or a stranger,
someone who does not understand my world,

my new biology. It's not your fault.
You are basically a pack animal.
Did you not think me one of you still,
I would be in danger.

I see you checking in on me,
my anxious nurse. I'm none too sure
what prognosis you think best.
Should I perfect

these neat new lungs,
we will cease to understand each other.
You will look into my gold, transparent eye

and see no soul. No soul like yours.

Should I reject them, however,
I might die, strapped to some machinery.
I can almost picture it.
Your funhouse face

nose and chin flattened against the window
of my aquarium
one finger tapping on the glass
like an exotic visitor.

Version 0.60

I'm in the middle of feeding Lucy when I find out.
Rafael says, *Your cousin Kathy called. Arturito fell,
and he's been in the hospital for two weeks. They
think this is it. I need to see him,* I say, even though
it's the beginning of the semester and I have no idea
how to handle it at work. Rafael makes it happen,
and $5000 later I'm in a rental driving to the hospital.

When I get there he is yellow. He looks already dead.
The trail of liver spots down his neck is the only thing
I can recognize as him. My cousin Randy is the optimist
—he's being moved to a less critical room and the
neurologist is hopeful. What they cannot understand
is why he seems to have lost his mind, unconscious
most of the time and incoherent the rest. There is no
way to get him to eat. I see Lois in the hallway
and for the first time she really looks ninety.

The next day Arturito recognizes me. *How is Panchito,*
he asks, as if this were a perfectly social visit.
He's well, I lie, and show him pictures of Lucy. *I
remember that day,* he says, looking at a picture of her
on the beach. He is confusing her with me. We bring
him more photo albums from home and play him songs
from Cuba. Sometimes he recognizes people and
even remembers lyrics to the tangos he so loved.

At night he takes to ripping off his clothes and trying
to set himself free of the tubes around his body,
the most dangerous of which is the Foley catheter
that he already pulled off once a long time ago,

the first time he fell and they had to drill holes
in his head to drain out the blood. Since then his
favorite activity was forcing you to touch them.
See? I have holes in my head, he'd say, as if they
were new. There's no such cure this time.

Four days pass and I must go back to work. I'm hopeful
because he's sat up and shaved his beard, the
familiar buzz of the electric razor taking me back
to those summer mornings he would stay with us
in Miami. I'd know he was up because of that buzz,
and every day with him was fun. The beach, dominoes,
movies, push rummy, later drinking martinis and
listening to Carlos Gardel and Eydie Gormé.
When I tell him I'm leaving he gestures c'mon, let's go,
as if I could take him with me.

It's an early Sunday morning when I get the call.
He passed away around 3 am, my cousin Donald
says. No family at all.

> *Que se quede el infinito sin estrellas*
> *O que pierda el ancho mar su inmensidad*
> *Pero el negro de tus ojos que no muera*
> *Y el canela de tu piel se quede igual.**

*"Piel Canela" lyrics by Bobby Capó

Version 0.61

Just last summer we were eating plátanos and making jokes.
You said, *we've been friends longer than most people
have been alive,* and we took a picture of the three of you
sitting under the cuckoo clock, three centuries almost
of gathered years.

I thought next summer would bring another round of café
and confusion, as your minds circled like hawks over memories
piled like dead bodies. *How depressing,* I had thought,
*this life so long and yet so dwindled now to a recurring
conversation about how many brothers have died and old
professors who used to bang their students and who can walk
better now that your back collapsed and Amanda's
feet are so stiff. What for, what for,* I thought,

just forty-two and already so close to death. I can feel it
every day when I wake up wooden as a puppet. Knees
cracking every time I have sex. *What for, what for,* these
decades like unraveled film reels that we
hold up to the light from the window and say
who's this? and what's that building there? and
I remember, I remember.

Well now, that's all over. Your friends are dead, one
broken hip after another, and you tell me you're next
as if this were no more to me than a matter of standing
by the register with groceries to check out. After we hang up
the phone I imagine you mulling the news over, last man
standing once more at the Battle of Old Baldy. How deep
is this wound in a heart already so scarred by ninety years
of news? I picture the pacemaker visible under the thin skin
of your left shoulder, the mechanical ticktock of your life.
The three of you, last summer, under the cuckoo clock.

Version 4.47

At 96, Arturito arrives in a wheelchair
pushed by a flight attendant. I usually
rush to meet him, but it is after 9/11,

and we must wait patiently by the gate
until he fully crosses. I have his namesake
in my arms, a seven-month-old dressed
in camo pants and an AC/DC t-shirt.

We thank the flight attendant and he leaves,
and I kneel and bend forward, putting the baby
on my uncle's lap. He laughs his bright
white smile (a dentist to the end) and I can see
small tears gathered in the corners of his eyes.

Can he walk yet? He asks, looking at the
stroller behind us, and I say no, but he can
crawl, a strange marine belly crawl, fists
under his chin and elbows out.

You'll be wheeling buddies, Rafael says,
and Arturito acquiesces to be rolled
to baggage claim.

Once we grab that old blue suitcase,
my uncle stands, and uses the spinning
cart to make it to the curb to get picked up.
I stroke the back of his head and kiss him
on his speckled cheek, and ask him,
What do you think? pointing my chin
at the baby. Arturito doesn't hear me,
the loud whirring of cars and taxis blurring
the sound in his hearing aid.

Instead he guides my fingers
to the top of his head, and says,
Here, touch here and here.
You feel the holes?

Version 0.70

Take them, my aunt, in her seventies, says,
giving me back all those pictures addressed
Con mucho cariño: the first-grader
with one pigtail tucked into the collar

of my shirt, the pious praying girl in
first-communion veil, the chunky kid in
cupcake *quinces* ballgown and the skinny
bride. *My children will only throw them out*

after I die. This is true. It has just
happened to her neighbor, who was also
her family's chronicler. In every
generation, there's one invisible

presence behind the camera. The one
who used to drive to Eckerd's after each
birthday party, or send away the rolls
in those bright-yellow discount envelopes.

Later, there was the one-hour shop, and
acid-free paper promising it would
always preserve each moment Kodak crisp.
I am my generation's keeper.

Now digital, I worry that all those pics
will one day degenerate into some
meaningless pixels like a bad Monet.
I used to back them up on floppies, those

defunct dinosaurs of the digital
stone age. Who's to say today's CDs and
USBs aren't tomorrow's laserdiscs,
and all my efforts at preservation

one viral download away from extinct?
It's not me I'd lose, of course. I've never

mastered the art of the timed tripod shot.
Even now when one of the pets dies and

I look for a picture to tape to the
tiny urn, I'm constantly shocked by my
absence in their short lives. There's my husband,
cuddling the calico in bed, giving Destiny a belly
rub in the yard. Where am I?

When my aunt dies, my cousins
despair at the boxes of pictures she
didn't have enough time to give away,
meticulously indexed by year and season:

Christmas 1997, Summer 1994, November
1954, 1955. Who is that posed by
the pier? Who is that sitting next to mom?
Who's the girl with the Mary Janes?

Is this a wedding, all these people in one room?
It's a snap decision. The night that the boxes
lie by the curb, there is a storm, and the wind
picks up the lids and index tabs,

showers the street in a ticker-tape
parade of mysterious events:
black-and-white babies genderless and bald
as seals, toothy kids in togas holding

diplomas, little girls in party gowns
and ruffled socks, stunned brides.
Their faces cling to the windshields of the
cars as they drive by and are wiped off.

I scan the pictures that she gave me into
my new 5G external hard drive, try
to remember who took them. They're mostly

professional portraits, school pictures, all

except for the one of my wedding. We
had no money for a photographer.
The shot of me getting out of the car
was taken by the best man's girlfriend.

They broke up soon after. My aunt's ashes
are divided among her children, who then
scatter them in places of their choosing:
near the sign in Key West that says Ninety

Miles to Cuba, behind the hotel in
Miami Beach where they spent their childhood
summers. You could say my aunt is now all
over Miami. Yet she is nowhere.

Version 1.70

Going through my father's things,
I find my parents' wedding picture.
Starting left to right, I can recognize
my uncle Sergio's first wife,
fat already and complacent
though everyone else is Max-Factor pretty,
lips dark and full, brows arched inquisitively.
Where is my uncle? Taking the picture, perhaps,
or maybe already working on the new wife.
Next to her I think might be my grandfather,
in sunglasses, poking his head out from behind
some woman I can't recognize, maybe also
his second wife. Two more people I don't know
and then my eldest aunt, noodle thin and slippery
in some satin gown down to her ankles, holding
a drink, even though now she insists she never
once touched the stuff. From right to left, I see
my two grandmothers, both in Victory Rolls, one
suited, one corsaged. In the center, my parents,
my mother in an enormous feathered hat and my dad
holding up a suit two sizes too big for his bones.

They are in some kind of library, some office,
some pre-revolutionary Cuba that in nine years
will take their furs and hats and change them
into ration cards, two miscarriages, and months
cutting sugar cane in a concentration camp
before all this gloss gets left behind. I will not even
see this picture for forty years, and when I do,
I will say *Who is this?* and *Who is this?*
in a language they can't understand.

Version 1.80

Getting rid of the daisy-wheel printer
turns out to be harder than I thought.
The man in the charity truck won't take it,
says *they wouldn't want it anywhere, Lady.*

But it still works, I assure him, realizing
that you'd somehow need to be able
to hook it up to a computer that spoke
the same Boolean dialect, or could ingest
that floppy pancake I managed to find
in the back of the closet, under a stack
of *TV Guides* with *Star Trek* covers.

Where would you even get
those endless scrolls of paper
with the holes down the sides
that would fan to the floor at 3 a.m.
after I'd finally finished that thesis
on *The Last of the Mohicans*?

DMP 240 is both too old and too new,
simultaneously a relic and a piece of junk.
It will sit a few weeks at the recycling facility
surrounded by VCRs and laserdisc players,
all in good working order. Someone might
pass by, wondering what language it could
speak, what it might say in an electric gasp:

> *What a trash*
> *To annihilate each decade.*

> *What a million filaments.*

I was able to convert the files
with every upgrade, but those printouts
with the perforated edges
and the scribbled comments of my old professors

are now toilet paper,
recycled into some more useful incarnation.
DMP 240 will be crushed
into Red Bull cans and milk jugs,
and I will grow old
rearranging books and DVDs on sagging shelves,
frantically trying to reassure myself:

> *These are my hands*
> *My knees.*
> *I may be skin and bone,*
>
> *Nevertheless, I am the same, identical woman.**

*Lines taken from Sylvia Plath's "Lady Lazarus."

Version 0.00

I imagine it was him and not my
mother, who felt love and obedience,
equal tensions in her solar plexus,
like a chord. Nor do I know who came first,
or who came after. He's never talked to
me about the night he sat on the front
stoop of that small house in old Havana
they once shared, looking out into the night,
finding nothing more that belonged to them.
Tendrils of hope already fastening
like seed pods to the heavy coats and quilts
packed for flight to Spain. I can see him, no
shoes, elbows on knees, always as supple
as sugarcane; sharp as a machete.

Version 1.40

Whitley finally sees Sara.
We drive across the state
to meet them halfway,
the two girls lulled to sleep
in the backseat.

She is all giggles and hugs
when we reunite in the parking lot,
this once nurse who became
a friend. We exchange news,
she coos over the girls, we

take pictures. Once we settle
into our lunch, we find ourselves
complaining about Sara's vomiting
and Lucy's rampant jealousy.

The cramped two rooms in which
we live, the kids' toys all over
the floor, the closet overflowing
with clothes. The midnight

feedings and screamings.
How it sometimes feels like
too much. "Thank God it
wasn't three, right?" she says, and

at first it doesn't register, I don't
even respond. Then on the way home
L'esprit de l'escalier takes over

and I imagine a dead silence
falling over the table like
a heavy blanket, Whitley

turning pink, then red, then purple,
babbling with shame, big fat tears

running down her face until it's me
that comforts her, *don't worry, I know
what you meant.*

In another version the blanket
does not fall but I say *Excuse me?*
and Whitley's face freezes as she
realizes what's she's said, and then
it goes pretty much the same, with
the purple face and big fat tears.
Rafael doesn't even hear the comment,
and I seethe the rest of the day.

Is this why my son died?
Because I didn't have enough room,
or enough stamina? Was I so weak
that God cut him off like an extra limb?

I fantasize again about calling her,
even now saying *You really hurt me
when you said* but I don't. In this

reality I don't. I don't explain the months
of silence, the tiny revenges like
not sending a Christmas card.

In this version I am a coward, and
my son is dead, and there is no
room in the closet for something
so small as shame, so stupid as regret.

Version 0.14

When I am 14 my mother gets mugged
in the parking lot of the Pizza Hut.
It's the smash-and-grab era,
only this time something goes wrong—
the guy has a construction hammer,
and gets my mother in the face rather
than breaking her window.

The Pizza Hut manager calls the police,
but my mother runs away, blood dripping
down her face, thinking that in her purse
is her driver's license with our home address
and it being summer I am by myself.
She doesn't realize the house keys are
still with the car keys in the ignition.

When she shows up I am still asleep,
having stayed up all night reading
like I used to do every summer,
the house quiet, my imagination reeling.

She comes in screaming, blood
covering her face and shirt.
Somehow I piece together what's happened
and realize that she is hysterical.
I drive her to the hospital even though
I have barely learned to drive yet.

They immediately put her on a morphine pump
and I realize the severity of the situation.
They will have to reconstruct her cheekbone
and her nose. I become annoyed
when the nurse comes in to ask her
medical history. My mother goes back too far,

all the way to Cuba and her bad circulation
and her three kidneys and the twins she

lost in line to get my grandmother some
yogurt. *I was five months along*, she says,
crying, *It was a boy and a girl.* I can see

the nurse losing patience and I'm embarrassed.
I try to explain to my mother that what the nurse
wants to know is if she's on any medication
right now. My mom looks at me and says,
This is my only daughter. She is amazing.

Version 1.50

I am dressing for church
when my mother comes into the room
and says my father can't breathe.

I find him gasping for air
seated on the edge of the bed,
unable to speak.

We call 911 for what seems like
the twelfth time since he retired.
I already know the drill—while they
get here I put on my jeans and my
trusty sweater, take the big bag,
make sure I've got his ID and
medical card. It's always the same
tall paramedic who once
begged him to go for my sake
when I was crying and he was
refusing to go even though he
had a fever of 104, chills, and
couldn't stand. *Just let me sleep.*

This time there is no such protest.
He arrives at the hospital
unconscious, his lungs full of fluid.
Something wrong with his heart.

They pump him dry and fix him up
and spend three days running tests—
he is inexplicably well, even though
he weighs less than I do and trembles
when he coughs. They slough him off.

I've spent all three days in an armchair
at the foot of his bed, telling the nurses
his medical history and the medicines
he takes. I correct him when he says

I feel just fine and tell them about
the coughing and the swaying when
he walks to the bathroom, the constant,
inexplicable vertigo. In between these
visits he talks to me, stories I've
heard before, but not from him.
How he'd wanted to study accounting
but his father had forced him into
the family business, the bakery
that is now for soldiers only. He tells
me the story of how he and his
eldest sister put their little brother
Manolo in the garbage because
they didn't want him. He spends
the whole day talking.

I just sit there and listen,
thinking he is talking more to himself
than to me. I share no stories of my own.

When the discharge papers come
I help him dress. He makes me pull
his shoestrings so tight I worry
they'll cut off circulation to his feet.
He says to me, *You know the one thing
that's been good about all this is
how I've gotten to know you better.*

When the wheelchair comes
I follow behind, carrying the big bag
full of diapers and toiletries
no one ever knows what to do with.

Version 1.51

It's after a pulmonologist's visit
that he tells me about the thousands
he has won and given away
to other people who *really need it.*

Meanwhile, I am giving him $5 a day
just to gamble, and scrambling to pay
this credit card with the other. I tell him
he won't see another penny from me
and we get into a huge argument
with phrases like *the least you could
have done* and *lo que te pasa a ti es
que eres un vividor* which has no
translation in English closer than "you're
a mooch," nothing even close to how
offensive it is to call your own father
un vividor.

When I stop giving him his daily $5
he stops leaving the house, sits
seething on his lazy boy *that I paid for*
watching the giant flatscreen tv *that I paid for*
and the special sports package channels
that I pay for every month.

This is when he starts scheming about
cashing in his life insurance. After I rip
the curtain off the door, I am able to pay
all the bills at once, and guilt sets in—
when I watch him shuffling from the lazy boy
to the bathroom and back all day long
in his red checkered pajamas and shoddy
slippers. He barely eats dinner and goes
to sleep. He is thinner and thinner.

I wonder: *Is it possible for someone to disappear?
Just evaporate?* One day we find his glasses

in the crook of the sofa and we suddenly realize
he's been gone for quite some time. When
was the last time anyone spoke to him?
No one remembers. How long does it take
to notice someone's dying? 26 days?

Version 1.52

For my father's birthday
I decide to make amends.
I kneel in front of him on the lazy boy
and talk to him like a child. *Look,*
I don't want to give you money
for your birthday. I want to go out

to dinner as a family and have
a nice time. Our family
has a history of disastrous dinners,
plates taken in their entirety and
slammed into the garbage, tears,
screaming. We are good at this.

Friday is his birthday and he showers,
shaves, dresses up nice. The smell
of 4711 wafts all the way to our side
of the house. The shaving does not
go well—between his sagging skin
and shaking hands, his face is a mess.

,
But I've got a secret: an electric
razor I've gotten him for Christmas.
A *real* present, not a fifty inside a card
signed by the girls. He's asked me
to shave him many times, but I'm
also scared of his sagging skin and
my shaky hands.

We've found a pizza place at the mall
that offers vegan cheese. We all sit
in a big table in the corner, the one
I've always wanted, with the big,
rambunctious family, and a baby
covered in cheese. This time,

This time it's us. We give him a beer

and we have *a great time.* We go home
and sing Happy Birthday! and sit around
the table eating vegan chocolate cake.

We go to bed and I relish the electric
razor in the drawer, the plan to give him back
his five dollars.

Version 2.80

When the discharge papers come
I ask to speak to the head nurse.
*How is it possible that they are
discharging my father when
they have no idea what caused
this episode?*

*Ma'am, there's nothing we can do;
all his tests have come back negative
and all the doctors have signed off
on him.*

*The hell there isn't. I want to speak
to the cardiologist right now.*

*Ma'am, the discharge instructions
say he needs to follow-up with his
own cardiologist—*

*Yes, but the cardiologist here says
he has a little bit of fluid around his
heart—*

*Which is probably due to his COPD.
You are also to follow-up with his
regular pulmonologist.*

I give up because he just so happens
to have an appointment to see his
regular pulmonologist this Tuesday,
who says *His lungs are clear.*

*Then why does he have fluid
around his heart?*

*COPD doesn't cause that.
He needs to go see his cardiologist.*

I'm sorry, ma'am but there are no
appointments till January.

But you don't understand, this is
an emergency . . . .

If it's an emergency then you need
to hang up and dial 911.

I look at my father playing with
the twins, and he doesn't seem
to be in any distress. His breathing
is normal; his birthday is coming,
and I have plans for a pizza party.

Alright, when is the next available
appointment?

I can fit you in Monday, January
20, at one o'clock.

Okay, I'll take it.

Version 3.80

I'm sorry, ma'am but there are no
appointments till January.

But you don't understand, this is
an emergency . . . .

If it's an emergency then you need
to hang up and dial 911.

It's not that kind of an emergency.
The paramedics wouldn't take him
He got kicked out of the hospital.

Then he is fine.

He is not fine, he has fluid around
his heart. He needs to see Dr. Diego
before the end of the week.

It's Christmas, ma'am, the doctor
is on vacation with his family.

But surely he's left someone behind;
the office isn't closed.

The RN's calendar is full. Again,
if this is an emergency . . . .

I look at my father playing with Lucy
and Sara , and he doesn't seem
to be in any distress. His breathing
is normal; his birthday is coming,
and I have plans for a pizza party.

I relent, I relent, I relent.

Version 1.54

Two days after the pizza party
it's Sunday and my mother again
comes in as I'm getting ready for mass:
Your father can't breathe.

When I get to his bedroom I find him
lying on his side on the bed, breathing
shallowly, staring out into nowhere.
Rafael is already calling 911.

I go put on my jeans and my trusty
sweater, take the big bag, make sure
I have his driver's license and insurance
card. *Here we go again.* A few seconds
before the paramedics arrive, I sit
by him and stroke his back. He does
not move nor notice me.

They haul him away on the bedsheet,
using it like a hammock to carry him
to the gurney on the porch. I'm
already in the front seat of the ambulance.

They lose his pulse as soon as they
get him in and start CPR. I watch
his left arm, with the black watch,
thin as a twig, slip out from under
the sheet. *It doesn't look good,*
Rafael says from the street.

The ride is short but long. We run
when we arrive. They put him
under a huge machine that makes
him flop like a fish. *You might not
want to see this,* a nurse says,
attempting to close the curtain.
I watched my son die. I can see this.

He doesn't come back.

He can still hear you, the nurse says,
talk to him, and I do, I whisper things
in his ear, I stroke his curly head.
They leave me alone with him again.
This time no priest comes.
I shut his eyes.

Version 1.55

Papi's funeral is across the street
from the casino where he gambled
our lives away. You can see the neon
Magic City sign from the window of
the parlor. This is sort of by design.
This funeral home was the only one
willing to help us bury Arturo no. 2,
since legally only fetuses 21 weeks
or older are allowed to be buried.
Back then I was working and we
had more money, so we went ahead
and made arrangements for all of us.
I had imagined this moment many times.

I pick the wrong shoes and hobble
the whole night, trying to make out
who is whom and whom to talk to
and who's on first and who's on second,
until I decide to just take them off. I imagine
how horrified my father would be at someone
barefoot at a funeral, he who always
wore a suit to such things, the suit
he's being buried in.

It's a modest crowd, but nevertheless
the four of us are alone by ten, Lucy
and Sara having stayed home with
Rafael's sister and mother. Though
we have the parlor till midnight,
I'm the one that says, *let's go.*

Before I do I put his Christmas card
in his coat pocket. It's a custom card
with a picture of the girls as Disney's
Elsa and Anna, and inside it says,
Ya no quiero pelear mas.
Someone's shaved him well, again,

like that nurse back in the hospital,
who took a single blade and stretched
his skin with such patience and precision.
With tenderness.

The following morning Rafael asks
the hearse driver to circle the casino
before heading off to the cemetery.
It's corny and it's weird. I dropped
him off so many times here after
he stopped driving. He used to hate it,
preferring to take the bus. I still have
one of his voicemails *It's raining too
hard, come pick me up.*

Version 1.60

We do not visit Papi's grave
for a long time. The electric
shaver goes back to Amazon.
The Christmas tree comes down.
The COVID-19 pandemic locks
us in for months. Sara turns two.

And then it's June, and two years
since Arturito no. 3 died, and we
decide to go. We have to wear
masks and gloves because of
the pandemic, but this time,
when I place my gloved hand
on his headstone, I feel something.
I sob silently. We move on to

Arturito no, 2, and then we get
lost trying to find Papi's grave.
I try to orient myself by the mausoleum,
and I finally find the right hill.
Rafael had asked me quickly on the
phone, *What do you want it to say
on the headstone*? And there it
is, the first thing that came to my mind.
Beloved husband, father, friend.

Here I feel nothing, but when my
mother hugs me, we sob together.
I think of how daunting it must be
to know that the empty space on
that plaque will one day have her
name, and some hasty words again.

And then I remember: Our plots,
Rafael's and mine, are right beside.
I am also standing on my own grave.

They've planted a red flowering tree
nearby. It looks like it might grow
to be quite big. Lucy and Sara
will have no trouble finding us.

Version 2.90

It's been years now
since my parents died,
and now it's Rafael and I
who are the grandparents.

Lucy grows up to be a doctor,
a cardiologist. She marries
the son of an old friend, and
they have twins, both boys.
She names them after my
father and her brother—
Francisco and Arturo.

Sara grows up to be a commercial
architect. She's known for buildings
that appear to wobble but don't fall.
She's a bohemian type, dresses
in bandanas and goes barefoot.
She has two little girls, Lucia
and Sonia, for my mom.

Somehow I have trouble imagining
what Arturo will finally be.
He drops out of college to paint,
then meets a girl he follows to Morocco.
When he comes back he's unshaven
and skinny as a string, heartbroken.
He shuffles around in his sweatpants,
watching tennis on TV.

On Thanksgiving we are a crowd—
almost a full dozen. The kids stayed
vegan. The Tofurky takes center
stage, and then we all pass around
the plates. Lucy's hair darkened
to a soft brown, and Sara and Arturo's
more a dirty blond. Their kids

look nothing like me, but they call
out *grandma! grandma!* always
wanting something—another piece
of pie, a glass of water. I can't
but stand and watch them.

Rafael's eyes catch mine. It is one of
those moments that stretches time.
Here we are, we say to each other
without words.

And then the moment's gone,
little Lucy going up to Rafael
and hugging his knees. *Pop-Pop,
Pop-Pop, carry me.*

Additional Acknowledgments

To God, Who, though we may not grasp His plan, always does what is best for us; to my mother, who was by my side at every moment, day or night; to my father, who was a great babysitter and the best father and grandfather one could ever hope for; to my husband, the only person who could ever understand the depth of my grief; to my granduncle Arturito, who was not just a grandfather figure to me, but also my best friend; to the members of the St. Dominic Church and Our Lady of Lourdes Academy communities, who held me up with prayer and so much more; to the staff at South Miami Hospital, who saved my daughter's life; to Shara McCallum, who gave me permission to write; to Geoffrey Philp and Vasiliki Katsarou, for their kind words and encouragement; to Finishing Line Press, who twice now has given my work an audience; to Ruben, who, though he will never read this book, will always have my gratitude; to Susan, Karina, Veronica, Eddy, Sarah, and Henry, who helped pick up the pieces, and to Dr. Freeman, who put them back together; to my Arturitos, the ones that never got to be and the one who lived just long enough to become a part of our family forever; and lastly to Lucy and Sara, who even in the midst of pain can bring me joy. I hope this book might one day help them understand, and remember.

Celia Lisset Alvarez was born in Madrid, Spain to Cuban parents fleeing from Fidel Castro's communist regime. After a four-year sojourn in Spain, the family immigrated to Miami, where they took root. Alvarez received an MFA in Creative Writing from the University of Miami, where she met fellow poet and professor Rafael Miguel Montes. They married in 1996, and she proceeded to work as an adjunct professor of English and creative and scientific writing at several south Florida universities. Frustrated by the lack of opportunities at the college level, Alvarez turned to teaching high school in 2014 at the renowned all-girls high school, Our Lady of Lourdes Academy. In the intervening years, she published two chapbooks of poetry, *Shapeshifting* (Spire Press, 2006) and *The Stones* (Finishing Line Press, 2006). Her stories and poems have appeared in numerous journals and anthologies, most recently in *How to Live on Other Planets: A Handbook for Aspiring Aliens* (Upper Rubber Boot Books, 2015) and *Adanna Literary Journal. Multiverses* (Finishing Line Press, 2021) is her first full-length collection. It is based on a harrowing four years of her life, in which she suffered two miscarriages, the death of her beloved grand-uncle Arturo, the death of her son, Arturo (named after her uncle), who was born prematurely and died after only 26 days, and the sudden death of her father. She is currently the editor of *Prospectus: A Literary Offering*, and lives with her husband, daughters Lucy and Sara, her mother, Sonia, and their dog, Maggie.

CPSIA information can be obtained
at www.ICGtesting.com
Printed in the USA
FSHW011045180521
81546FS